PENTAB
THEAT

presents the world premiere of

Blue
Sky

Clare Bayley

First performance at Hampstead Theatre Downstairs, London
on 24 October 2012

Blue Sky

Clare Bayley

The Company

Cast (in order of appearance)

JANE	Sarah Malin
RAY	Jacob Krichefski
ANA	Dominique Bull
MINA	Manjeet Mann

Director	Elizabeth Freestone
Designer	Naomi Dawson
Lighting Designer	Johanna Town
Sound Designer	Adrienne Quartly
Costume Supervisor	Chris Cahill

Production Manager	Cressida Klaces
Company Stage Manager	Helen Gaynor
Deputy Stage Manager	Altan Reyman
Deputy Stage Manager (Book Cover)	Sam Eccles
Set Builder	Andy Stubbs

Blue Sky was developed with the support of the National Theatre Studio.

Following the initial run at Hampstead Theatre, Pentabus Theatre takes *Blue Sky* to Sherman Cymru.

Cast

SARAH MALIN Jane
Theatre credits include: *Here Lies Mary Spindler, Macbeth, Macbett, The Penelopiad* (RSC); *Iphigenia* (National Theatre); *Marianne Dreams* (Almeida); *The Cherry Orchard* (English Touring Theatre); *Pericles* (Lyric Hammersmith); *The Book of David* (The Really Useful Group); *Twelfth Night* (Imaginary Forces); *The Norman Conquests* (Clwyd Theatr Cymru); *Grimm Tales* (Scarborough); *Ring* (Soho); *No Way Out* (ATC); *Madness in Valencia, Hecuba* (Gate); *The Merchant of Venice, Dracula* (Sherman Cymru); *World on Fire, David Copperfield* (New Vic); *Dangerous Corner, Dead Wood* (Watermill).

Television credits include: two series of *The Knock, Every Silver Lining, Wire in the Blood, Silent Witness, Guardian, The Law, The Bill, EastEnders* and eight months in *Emmerdale*.

JACOB KRICHEFSKI Ray
Theatre credits include: *The Great Extension* (Theatre Royal Stratford East); *Market Boy* (National Theatre); *The Tempest* (York Theatre Royal/Sprite); *Hamlet, The Seagull* (The Factory); *Lucifer Saved* (Finborough).

Television credits include: *A Touch of Frost, Silent Witness, Sex Traffic, The Bill, Maisie Raine*.

Radio credits include: *The Kiss* (BBC Radio 4).

DOMINIQUE BULL Ana
Dominique trained at Central School of Speech and Drama on the Collaborative and Devised Acting course. Since graduating she has worked in Europe, India and Australia and most recently in London on the core team of *You Me Bum Bum Train*. Credits include: *Almost, Maine* (Cathaayatra); *The Vagina Monologues* (Subiaco Arts Centre); *Lapse* (ARTillery festival); *Macbeth* (Out of Cocoon Theatre); *Romeo and Juliet* (Shakespeare's Globe).

MANJEET MANN Mina
Theatre credits include: *Born Again, Endless Light* (Kali/Southwark Playhouse); *The Project* (Birmingham Rep); *Counted* (Look Left Look Right); *Transmissions Festival* (Birmingham Rep); *James and the Giant Peach, The BFG* (Polka); *That Pesky Rat* (Soho); *When Amar Met Jay* (Lyric Hammersmith); *The Duel* (Newhampton Arts); *Koba, Man of Steel* (Alexandra, Birmingham); *A Midsummer Night's Dream, The Crucible* (Ellen Terry Theatre, Coventry); *Prospero's Island* (Midland Actors Theatre); *Subverse* (Theatre503).

Television credits include: *EastEnders, Derailed, DCI Banks, Primeval*.

Film credits include: *The Score, The Plague, Almost Adult*.

Manjeet was a member of the BBC Radio Rep Company for six months after winning the Norman Beaton Competition, recording numerous plays for BBC Radio 3 and 4. She has since recorded many more radio plays.

Creative Team

CLARE BAYLEY Writer
Clare Bayley's play, *The Container*, was first produced in Edinburgh 2007 where it won a Fringe First and the Amnesty International Award prior to a subsequent production at the Young Vic in 2009. Her English version of *The Enchantment* was produced at the Cottesloe auditorium of the National Theatre in 2007. Clare wrote *The Woman Who Swallowed a Pin* for Southwark Playhouse. For Paines Plough, *They Said, We Said* for *Come to Where I'm From* at Chipping Norton Theatre in 2012.

Clare also adapted *The Container* into a radio play (Bona Broadcasting for BBC Scotland) and her other recent radio credits include *Portobello Beach* (Absolutely Productions) and *In the Van* (Bona Broadcasting for BBC Radio 4).

Blue Sky was written while on attachment at the National Theatre Studio.

ELIZABETH FREESTONE Director
For Pentabus: *Stand Up Diggers All* by Phil Porter and *The Hay Play* by Nell Leyshon. Other directing credits include: *The Rape of Lucrece*, *Here Lies Mary Spindler*, *The Tragedy of Thomas Hobbes* and *The Comedy of Errors* (all for the RSC). *Endless Light* (Kali/Southwark Playhouse); *The Duchess of Malfi, Dr Faustus, The School for Scandal, Volpone* (Greenwich Theatre); *Romeo and Juliet* (Shakespeare's Globe); *Top Girls, Three Sisters, Night Must Fall* (RWCMD); *Skellig, Rocket Fuel, No Place Like Home* (OnO Theatre); *The Travels of the Three English Brothers* (British Museum); *A Gloriously Mucky Business* (LAMDA/Lyric Hammersmith); *The Water Harvest* (Theatre503); *Left on Church Street* (Bridewell) and *The Moment You Stop* (Liverpool Playhouse Studio). Elizabeth was Associate Director on *The Caucasian Chalk Circle* (National Theatre) and has been a Staff Director at the RSC, the National, the Royal Court, Hampstead and Soho. She trained at Rose Bruford College and the National Theatre Studio.

NAOMI DAWSON Designer
Design includes: *Monkey Bars* (Traverse); *Y Storm* (Theatr Genedlaethol Cymru); *King John* (RSC); *Keep Breathing, King Pelican, Speed Death of the Radiant Child* (Drum Theatre Plymouth); *Speechless* (Shared Experience, UK tour); *Belongings* (Hampstead/Trafalgar Studios); *In Praise of Love* (Theatre Royal); *Landscape* & *Monologue* (Ustinov); *Love and Money* (Malmo Stadsteater); *Amerika, Krieg der Bilder* (Staatstheater Mainz); *Scorched* (Dialogue/Old Vic Tunnels); *The Typist* (Sky Arts/ Riverside Studios); *The Gods Weep* (RSC/ Hampstead); *The Glass Menagerie* (Shared Experience/Salisbury Playhouse); *Rutherford and Son* (Northern Stage); *Three More Sleepless Nights* (National Theatre); *The Container, The Pope's Wedding, Forest of Thorns* (Young Vic); *Can Any*

Mother Help Me? (Foursight/UK tour); *Amgen: Broken* (Sherman Cymru); *If That's All There Is* (Lyric); *State of Emergency, Mariana Pineda* (Gate); *...Sisters* (Gate/Headlong); *Stallerhof, Richard III, The Cherry Orchard, Summer Begins* (Southwark Playhouse); *Phaedra's Love* (Young Vic/Barbican Pit); *Different Perspectives* (Contact, Manchester); *Market Tales* (Unicorn); *Attempts on Her Life, Widows, Touched* (BAC); *In Blood, Venezuela, Mud, Trash, Headstone* (Arcola); *A Thought in Three Parts* (Burton Taylor).

JOHANNA TOWN Lighting Designer
Theatre credits include: *Straight, The Pride, That Face* (Sheffield); *Moon on a Rainbow Shawl* (National Theatre); *The Norman Conquests* (Liverpool); *Medea, Romeo and Juliet* (Headlong); *Blue Heart Afternoon, Lay Down Your Cross* (Hampstead); *What the Butler Saw, Betrayal, Speaking in Tongues, Fat Pig* (West End); *Some Like it Hip Hop* (ZooNation); *Charged* (Soho); *Miss Julie, Beautiful Thing, Private Lives, The Glass Menagerie, A Raisin in the Sun* (Royal Exchange); *Man in the Middle* (Theatre503); *The Deep Blue Sea/Nijinsky* (Chichester); *Fatherland* (Gate); *The Tragedy of Thomas Hobbes* (RSC); *Les Liaisons Dangereuses* (Salisbury); *Haunted* (Royal Exchange/New York); *Romeo and Juliet, The Importance of Being Ernest* (Lyceum, Edinburgh). Productions for Out Of Joint include: *Our Country's Good, Bang Bang Bang, Dreams of Violence, Our Lady of Sligo, The Permanent Way* and *King of Hearts*. Extensive work with the Royal Court includes: *My Name is Rachel Corrie, Rhinoceros, The Arsonists* and *My Child*.

ADRIENNE QUARTLY Sound Designer
Theatre credits include: *The Astronaut's Chair, Grand Guignol, Nostalgia, Horse Piss for Blood* (Drum Theatre Plymouth); *The Roundabout Season* (Paines Plough); *Rings of Saturn* (Katie Mitchell, Halle Kirk, Cologne); *The Importance of Being Earnest* (Rose, Kingston/Hong Kong Arts Festival); *You Can't Take it With You* (Told by an Idiot, Royal Exchange); *Farewell to the Theatre* (Rose, Kingston); *And The Horse You Rode In On* (Told by an Idiot, Barbican); *Chekhov in Hell* (Soho/Drum Theatre Plymouth); *Fräuline Julie* (Katie Mitchell, Schaübuhne); *Stockholm* (Frantic Assembly/Sydney Theatre Company); *Thomas Hobbes/Mary Spindler* (RSC); *The Container* (Young Vic); *365* (National Theatre of Scotland); *Woyzeck* (St. Ann's Warehouse, New York);*The Painter* (Arcola); *Reykjavik* (Roundhouse); *My Zinc Bed, Private Fears; Just Between Ourselves* (Royal & Derngate, Northampton); *93.2FM* (Royal Court); *The Fastest Clock in the Universe* (Hampstead).

Composing credits include: *The Tragedy of Thomas Hobbes* (RSC); *The Duchess of Malfi, Faustus, Volpone, The School for Scandal* (Stage on Screen); *The Painter, Enemy of the People* (Arcola).
www.adriennequartly.com

CHRIS CAHILL Costume Supervisor

Costume-design credits include: *Our Country's Good* (Nuffield, Southampton); *Going Straight* (national tour); *Mercy* (Soho); *Tommy* (national tour); *The Honeymoon Suite* (Royal Court); *Kingfisher Blue* (Bush); *An Englishman Abroad* (Bridewell); *Independent State* (Sydney Opera House Studio).

Costume supervisor on recent productions, including: *Cyrano de Bergerac* (Broadway); *The School for Scandal* (Theatre Royal Bath); *Tender Thing*, *King John*, *Marat Sade*, *Macbeth*, *Macbett*, *The Gods Weep*, *Days of Significance*, *The Tragedy of Thomas Hobbes*, *I'll be the Devil*, *Venus and Adonis* and *Tynan* (RSC); *Six Characters in Search of an Author* (Chichester); *Tiger Country* (Hampstead); *When the Rain Stops Falling* (Almeida); *Piaf* (Vaudeville); *Three Days of Rain* (Apollo); *Gypsy*, *The King and I*, *Molly Sweeney* (Curve, Leicester); *Sing Your Heart Out for the Lads* (National Theatre); *Sacrifice* (Welsh National Opera); *Into the Little Hill* (Linbury Theatre).

Acknowledgements

Special thanks to:

Rosie Armstrong, Freecycle, Morgan Reece, Oliver Smith, Lyric Hammersmith and Wolverhampton Halfpenny Green Airport

PENTABUS THEATRE

Pentabus believes in making theatre that examines who we are, connects people and ideas, and brings communities together.

Based on a farm in rural Shropshire, we produce plays that dig deep into the psyche of the English countryside. Our shows are playful, political and compassionate, offering rural audiences work that is made especially for, and speaks directly to them. We then take these plays on the road, touring around the country, telling stories that are born locally, but resonate nationally.

Our Radical Rural season, running throughout 2012, has seen us commission three new plays by three award-winning writers – Clare Bayley, Nell Leyshon and Phil Porter. We have invited these playwrights to respond politically and theatrically to the rural world, reclaiming the countryside as a place of protest and discourse, upheaval and dissent.

Pentabus was founded in 1973 and originally toured new work to five counties in the West Midlands, hence PENT (five) and BUS (touring). Productions in those early years included shows in fields, barns, village halls and pubs. As time went on the company extended its reach to include national and international projects.

Today we are proud to be an NPO and tour new work all over the country. We pioneer new forms of storytelling and examine contemporary culture through a rural prism. Recent productions include *Stand Up Diggers All* at the Latitude Festival exploring the links between the Occupy movement and the English Civil War, *The Hay Play* looking at the impact of such festivals on local communities, and *For Once* (at Hampstead last year) about young people and road accidents in the countryside.

Our productions turn up at festivals, in fields, in village halls and in theatres, reaching our audience wherever they may be. In fact, our mission can be summed up as: we tell the most exciting stories in the most surprising ways.

Supported using public funding by
ARTS COUNCIL ENGLAND
LOTTERY FUNDED

'The excellent Pentabus' *Guardian*

Pentabus Theatre, Bromfield, Ludlow, Shropshire, SY8 2JU

www.pentabus.co.uk

info@pentabus.co.uk

'Follow us' and 'Like us' on Twitter and Facebook

Join our mailing list

Why not visit our website at www.pentabus.co.uk and join our mailing list.
Alternatively fill in a join our mailing list card and return it to us by post.

Pentabus Staff

Elizabeth Freestone	Artistic Director
John Moreton	Executive Director
Thomasina Carlyle	Administrative Producer
Sarah Hughes	Administrator
Lynda Lynne	Bookkeeper
Heather Perez	Cleaner
Liz Hyder	Press Officer

Associate Artists

Soutra Gilmour, Thusitha Jayasundera, Gary Owen

Board of Directors

Kate Organ (Chair), Mary Wells, Ed Collier, Elanor Thompson,
Debbie Kermode, Lyndsey Turner, Joseph Alford, Sean Holmes
and Alison Vermee

Philanthropists make things happen. All artists depend on the support of philanthropic patrons to achieve their creative ambitions. People are not, in the end, remembered for how they made their money, but for the good they did with it. From funding a van that enables us to tour to geographically isolated communities, to sponsoring a young writer to write their first play; there are numerous ways to make a difference.

We'd like to thank the following people for their support:

Pentabus Patrons

Patricia and Richard Burbidge OBE*
Viscount Windsor
The Hon Robert Windsor Clive
Sir David Hare
Tim and Penny Bevan
Vera and Geoff Unitt
Alan and Karen Grieve
Ripples Magazine
Mary and Colin Wells
David and Thelma Eccleshall
Anonymous donors

Pentabus is also grateful for the contributions of its other supporters this year:

Nick Warburton
SOLO International Ltd (Specialist Operations & Logistic Organisation Ltd)
Tony Trotter and Homebase
Ben Szreider and Eglo

Join our story by becoming a Pentabus Patron or Pentabus Supporter. Your support can help us continue a range of initiatives and projects benefiting audiences, communities and artists locally and across the UK.

Reach out and invest in talent. Encourage emerging artists. Get in touch with Thomasina at thom@pentabus.co.uk or on 01584 856564 to discuss ways in which you can make a lasting contribution to creative innovation and excellence.

Foreword

The play is set between January and May 2003.

In October 2001 a newspaper in Karachi alleged a man had been handed over to US troops and put on a private jet by men in black masks.

In 2008, despite previous denials, Foreign Secretary David Miliband admitted that US rendition flights had stopped on UK soil.

In April 2009 Barack Obama released the 'Torture Memos', revealing how George Bush and the CIA attempted to justify the use of torture ('enhanced interrogation techniques') and to circumvent the Geneva Conventions when dealing with detainees in the 'war on terror'.

Reprieve continues to collect evidence of the UK's complicity in torture.

http://www.aclu.org/accountability/released.html

Clare Bayley

BLUE SKY

Clare Bayley

For my mother,
who prefers to know the truth, however hard

Characters

JANE, *a woman in her forties*
RAY, *a man in his forties*
ANA, *Ray's daughter, late teens*
MINA, *a woman, thirties*

Acknowledgements

Thanks to Sebastian Born. Purni Morell. Helena Lymbery, and all the actors who took part in workshops at the National Studio. Stephen Grey, and his fascinating book *Ghost Plane*. Ben Jaffey at Blackstone Chambers. Stephen Lovell-Davis. Mick Sanders, and all the people we talked to at airports and about planes. As always, to Giles Smart at United Agents. To Chris, Felix and Laurie, with love. And above all to Elizabeth Freestone for her inspiration and faith.

C.B.

This text went to press before the end of rehearsals and so may differ slightly from the play as performed.

JANE *is working at her laptop. She looks up. The sound of planes.*

Scene One

January 2003. The perimeter fence. RAY *is standing watching planes, stamping his feet against the cold. When a plane comes in, he photographs it with a large lens. He has a bag with more equipment in, and other plane-spotters' kit.* JANE *enters. She watches* RAY *for a while, then waits until a plane has just landed, before moving in.*

JANE. Ray!

RAY. What are you doing here?

JANE. I phoned the house. Ana said I'd find you here.

RAY. Has something happened? Your mum…?

JANE. No, no. I just wanted to look you up.

RAY. It's great to see you. Hey.

What a surprise!

He tries to give her a kiss – his large lens gets in the way.

JANE. That's a very large lens you've got there, Ray.

RAY (*embarrassed*). Yeah, well – ah, it's a good one, yes.

JANE. And what's all this kit you've got here?

RAY. Oh, that's just some…

JANE. This one's even bigger!

RAY. Yes, that's for long-distance shots.

JANE. What's with the little ladder?

RAY. It's quite useful, to get up above the perimeter fence.

JANE. Ray, has this plane-spotting thing of yours got a bit out of hand?

RAY. No, it's just a...

If you think this is bad, you should see what some of the blokes have!

JANE. Really?

RAY. Oh yes. This is nothing compared to –

JANE. There's one coming in now, Ray. Don't miss it!

RAY. Never mind that. How are you?

JANE. But look, Ray. What is it?

RAY. Yes, that's a nice little Cessna. I think it's a Citation Mustang.

JANE. Something special?

RAY. They're about the only one of the very light jets to have an onboard toilet.

JANE. I'm glad I know that.

This is some serious equipment you've got here, Ray. Even your thermos is massive –

RAY. You must think I've turned into a bit of a –

JANE. That's a hell of a thermos, Ray. For an amateur.

RAY. I do sell some of my pictures, to specialist magazines.

JANE. Don't you still work at the garage?

RAY. I do roadside rescue nowadays. It gives me flexibility.

JANE. You're one of those blokes who you call when you break down?

RAY. Yes. This plane thing is just a hobby, really.

JANE. This is a funny little place, isn't it? I never knew it was here.

RAY. It's lovely – not like a big international airport. I know all the blokes who work here, it's very informal. You can get up really close. And if it's raining I can have a cup of tea with Pete in the control tower.

JANE. Look – there's one!

RAY. Never mind about that. It's good to see you!

You look just the same.

JANE. You're looking pretty fine yourself, Ray.

RAY. If I'd known you were coming, I'd have put on my best anorak.

JANE (*watching the plane*). What is that then?

RAY (*lining up his shot in spite of himself*). That's actually an aerobatic plane.

JANE. How do you know?

RAY. You see the wings? They go out from the fuselage at ninety degrees. Most small planes have wings at an angle, to give them greater stability.

JANE. Okay…

RAY. And this one hasn't got a nose wheel, just a small tail wheel.

JANE. Let's see. You pleased with that picture?

RAY. Not bad. Nice light.

JANE. And the tail number is clearly visible.

RAY. You've been doing your homework.

JANE. The tail number tells you where a plane is registered, right?

RAY. So suddenly you're interested in planes?

JANE. Yes. I am.

RAY. Get off it.

JANE. It's for a story I'm working on.

RAY. Oh. I see.

JANE. I've got a hunch that planes are going to be part of the puzzle.

RAY. Right.

A beat.

That's why you came to see me?

JANE. Kind of.

RAY. And I thought it was because of my pretty face.

JANE. That's always an added bonus with you, Ray.

RAY. You're a heartless bitch, Jane Simonds. So you're still at the newspaper?

JANE. No. No, I'm freelance now.

RAY. I thought that was a plum job.

JANE. I quit.

RAY. Jane...?

JANE. My editor didn't want to send me on the stories I wanted to do. Investigative journalism is falling apart, Ray. Nobody has the budget any more.

So I thought, sod it.

I'll go freelance.

RAY. How's that working out then?

JANE. I'm going to break this story on my own.

Then they'll beg me to come back. And I'll be able to dictate my terms.

RAY. Yeah? What's the story?

JANE. I'm still working on that bit.

RAY (*laughing*). I see.

JANE. The tail number – is it an international thing? Does it tell you where a plane comes from anywhere in the world?

RAY. I'm fine. Ana's fine. Thanks for asking.

JANE. Sorry, Ray.

How about I come round for dinner? We can catch up.

RAY. What – tonight? Now?

JANE. Why not? I'd love to see Ana. She sounds like a grown-up.

RAY. She is. She's doing a degree in Media Studies – she's just home for the Christmas holidays.

JANE. God! That counts as a degree now, does it? Why doesn't she just get a job on the *Western Daily Press*, like I did?

RAY. It'd be good for her to talk to you. The voice of experience.

JANE. And you can give me a crash course in plane-spotting.

RAY. I'm not a plane-spotter.

JANE. Oh no, of course not.

Just – some of your best friends are.

RAY. Go on then. I'll cook you supper, and then you can come up and have a look at my flight logs.

JANE. Now there's an offer.

RAY *leaves.* JANE *thinks she sees a figure or figures in the shadows.*

Scene Two

That night, at RAY's. RAY *bringing food to the table.* JANE *pours wine.*

JANE. Funny being in this house again. That conker tree – it's massive now. It's a proper tree.

RAY. When Mum died, I couldn't bear to sell the house.

JANE. Sorry I couldn't make it to the funeral. I was abroad.

RAY. I appreciated your letter.

JANE. She was good to me, your mum. Remember that night, when I ran here all the way from our house? It seemed such a long way down that lane in the pitch dark. But it's not so far really.

RAY. How are things – with your mum?

JANE. The Home's great. She's off my hands. Thank Christ.

RAY. I should visit her.

JANE. She won't know who you are. She doesn't know who I am.

RAY. I'm sorry.

JANE. I've got to clear out the house. I've left it long enough, but now I'm freelance, I need the money, frankly.

RAY. You could live there. We could be neighbours again.

JANE. Are you kidding? I need the city now. I need twenty-four-hour corner shops and a mobile-phone signal that doesn't cut out when you go into the hall. Out here you could just cease to exist.

Nobody can hear you scream.

ANA *enters, carrying laptop.*

ANA. Hi.

RAY. Here you are, Ana. This is –

JANE. I'm Jane. I think you were about two last time I saw you.

RAY. No – there was one time you came down, Ana must have been about five then.

JANE. That's right – you told me you wanted to be a barmaid when you grew up.

ANA. That dream came true – I'm working at The Plough.

JANE. The Plough?

ANA. It's the pub in the village. I do a bit of cash-in-hand there.

JANE. I used to work at The Plough.

ANA. Seriously?

JANE. It was a terrible dive. Do you still have to run the hot tap over the frozen prawns to make prawn cocktail?

ANA. They don't do food. Well, except for scratchings and crisps.

JANE. Just as well, probably.

ANA. It's just a holiday job. I'm studying journalism.

JANE. Being a barmaid would probably have been a more sensible career choice.

RAY. Jane!

ANA. Dad showed me some of your articles.

RAY. I always look out for your byline.

ANA. I've always wanted to write.

JANE. It seems weird to me that journalism's a degree. But I'm old-school. At least it gets you away from here.

ANA. I like it here.

JANE. Once I got away I never looked back.

ANA. I wouldn't abandon Dad.

JANE. I suppose you can study. No distractions.

ANA. I've got a blog.

ANA *opens her laptop to show* JANE.

JANE. Oh God! Now everyone's got their own blog, editors can just fill their pages with that kind of crap for free and nobody has to actually know anything. They just have to have an opinion.

ANA *closes her laptop.*

ANA. Online journalism is a way for the truth to get out when it wouldn't otherwise.

JANE. Bullshit!

RAY. Jane!

JANE. Well, how do we know what's the truth when it's completely anecdotal and unattributable?

ANA. What about the Baghdad blogger? Do you read him?

JANE. How do I know who he is? He could be a Saddam stoodge. He could be some little fantasist sitting in Telford making it all up.

RAY. I'm sure you can argue –

ANA. Okay so where are the journalists covering Iraq right now? They're all embedded with the army. We're going to get a really impartial, balanced view from them, aren't we?

RAY. I suppose Jane has a point – and you won't get paid for blogging.

ANA. It's not all about money, Dad!

JANE. It is if you're trying to earn a living.

ANA. The future of journalism's going to be more democratic, and web-based. Ordinary citizens can –

JANE. Citizen journalism is just another name for unverified, unresourced –

ANA. What if twenty people all give eyewitness reports of the same incident?

JANE. That can corroborate a well-researched, well-written –

ANA. And what if the proprietor of the newspaper doesn't want to publish that well-researched piece? What if the editor is taken out to lunch by powerful interests –

JANE. You're talking about eyewitness accounts.

But who's going to find out about the things that nobody sees? That nobody even knows are happening?

ANA. Sure. The trouble is, people like me don't tend to buy newspapers. They want information online.

I've got to go now I'm afraid.

She gets up, clears her plate. Starts texting.

RAY. Now?

ANA (*texting*). Yes, there's a party – I'll be back late.

RAY. That's a shame, I thought –

ANA (*texting*). Sorry, Dad.

RAY. Perhaps, Jane, you could…

JANE. Yes – if I can help. I don't know. Let me know.

ANA. Thanks. I'm taking the car, Dad.

RAY. Okay. Drive carefully.

ANA. Have a look at my blog, anyway.

JANE. What's it called? I'll take a look.

ANA. What's your email address?

JANE. Just write it down – here.

She gives ANA *a paper napkin and a pen.* ANA *writes it down on the napkin.* JANE *pockets it.*

ANA. See you later.

RAY. Bye, love.

> JANE *waves*. ANA *leaves*.

> Jesus, Jane. I only wanted you to give her a bit of
> encouragement.

JANE. Sorry. But you've got to be realistic.

RAY. She's just a kid.

JANE. She'll do well. She came right back at me. She's got
spirit.

RAY. Oh yes, no shortage of that.

JANE. Like her mum?

> What's wrong?

RAY. Oh – I worry.

JANE. What about?

RAY. Everything! Drugs. Nasty boyfriends. Pregnancy.

JANE. Ray! She's an adult.

RAY. She never talks to me any more. She spends all her time
on her bloody laptop.

JANE. Don't worry!

RAY. You get paranoid. You read an article, ten ways to tell if
your child's on drugs. And then you start seeing the clues in
everything she does.

JANE. Are you really worried about drugs?

RAY. No. But if you stare too hard at anything, you start seeing
things that aren't there.

JANE. Except in my case. When they are there – I just can't see
them.

RAY. When we were kids, our parents got to know what we
were up to – friends had to phone the house or call round.

Now it all goes on texts. Beep of a text. Rattle of the keyboard. Headphones on. Switching screens when you try and snatch a look.

JANE. If you're that curious, Ray, why don't you just have a look? This is it, is it – her laptop?

RAY. I couldn't do that.

JANE. Don't you know her password?

RAY. I mean, I just couldn't.

JANE. If it put your mind at rest...

RAY. I'd feel bad.

JANE. Want me to do it for you?

RAY. What?!

JANE. Just a quick look. Check her browsing history.

RAY. I'm not going to do that – I'm not that cheap!

JANE. Fair enough. Just offering.

So what is it with the planes, Ray?

RAY. Why do I like them?

JANE. Yeah.

RAY. I think it's the sheer beauty of the technology.

JANE. The engines, or the design?

RAY. Everything. They look so purposeful, even on the ground. But then when they're in the air –

JANE. You wish you were flying them?

RAY. No – it's just the noise, and the power –

JANE. Would you like to own one?

RAY. I'd never be able to afford it.

JANE. Look but don't touch?

RAY. When you see something really amazing, like a Vulcan, say – it just makes you feel… you want to go over and hug them. Sometimes it makes me want to cry.

JANE. Blimey, Ray.

RAY. I was driving back from a job once. It was late, almost dusk on a beautiful, summer evening. I decided to go past that little airfield.

So I was driving down this country road, right next to the runway. All the cow parsley was in flower, the swallows were skimming through the trees, there was a clear sky, the light was beautiful, kind of violet – and suddenly I heard this roar. I pulled over and a Vulcan came right over my head, massive and dark in the half-light, with its distinctive delta wing, like a moth – like a giant, roaring metal moth.

Honestly, I stood there watching, and there were tears running down my cheeks.

JANE (*moved*). Wow.

RAY. Yeah.

JANE. What's a Vulcan doing in a little airfield like that? They're the ones they used in the Falklands War, aren't they?

RAY. The military use it as well, from time to time.

JANE. I've got this tail number, Ray. And I want to find out where the plane went. Who owns it. Stuff like that.

RAY. Why are you interested in this plane?

JANE. Not for the reasons you are. How would I find that out?

RAY. People post all the flights on websites. All the info's out there, if you know where to find it.

JANE. Seriously?

He goes to his computer.

How do they do it?

RAY. With scanners.

JANE. What kind of scanners?

RAY. Hand-held devices. Like this one.

He shows her his scanner.

They read the ACARS signal. You download the data onto
your computer and it tells you the flight plan, arrival and
departure reports, the tail number – sometimes you can even
hear the pilot talking to the control tower.

JANE. And they allow that?

RAY. There's nothing illegal about it.

JANE. Why have you got one of these?

RAY. I got it off the internet. It was only about a hundred quid.

JANE. Can it tell you who owns the plane?

RAY. You can find that out by an internet search.

JANE. It's that easy? Isn't it a security risk?

RAY. We're harmless.

JANE. We?

RAY. So what's the story?

JANE. How long have you got?

RAY. Stay the night. If you like.

JANE. It's okay.

RAY. Can't be very nice for you in that empty house.

JANE. That's true.

RAY. I'm not trying to –

JANE. No, I didn't think –

RAY. You can kip on the sofa.

JANE. Okay. Thanks.

Are you seeing anyone, Ray, at the moment?

RAY *shakes his head.*

RAY. You?

JANE. There's someone. He's abroad most of the time.

 We meet up periodically, and make each other unhappy.

 So go on. Show me.

 He goes to the computer.

RAY. Okay. Pick an airport. Any airport.

JANE. I don't know. Luton?

RAY. Luton. *Voilà.*

 She looks at him.

JANE. That's it?

RAY. That's all the flights in and out of Luton Airport today.

JANE. Okay… G199BA. CL60. EGGW. LIRA.

 She shrugs helplessly.

RAY. Yeah, 10.01.03 16.10 GMT.

 You see N199BA, that's the tail number. CL60, that's the
 type of plane, a nice little engine that'll have. It left Luton
 Airport, bound for Rome Ciampino at ten past four on 10th
 January.

JANE. Where does it say Luton?

RAY. EGGW, that's the code for Luton.

 Amazing, isn't it?

JANE. How far back does this go?

RAY. How far back d'you want to go? Two years ago? Three?
 It's all here.

JANE. This is incredible, Ray. I can't believe it – you're an
 oracle.

RAY. Right. We'll do a search for you. What's the tail number?

JANE. N829MG.

RAY. N? American-registered, then.

JANE. Is it?

RAY. So what is this story then? Some kind of celebrity scandal?

JANE. Not exactly. It was spotted in May in Karachi.

RAY. Karachi? Okay. Well, we can find all the flights logged in and out of Karachi this year. We can narrow it down to May...

JANE. This is amazing.

RAY. Tell me what it's about. You're being very cagey.

JANE. It's just a hunch, really.

All I know is, there was an incident in Karachi. I saw a tiny piece about it in the paper. An airport employee witnessed a man being bundled into a private jet by men in black ski masks. He got the tail number, and contacted a local reporter. Turns out the prisoner was a terror suspect. But nothing more is known about where he went or where he is now.

RAY. Okay.

JANE. And I can't stop thinking about it. Something definitely happened – but nobody knows what, or why – or where he is now.

RAY. And that's all you've got to go on?

JANE. I mean, people don't just disappear. Somebody knows.

Then I thought about the plane. I thought I must be able to trace the plane.

And then I thought of you.

RAY. So, who do you think those masked men were?

JANE. I think they could be CIA.

RAY (*dubious*). Really?

Why would they use private jets? Think of the cost. Surely they'd use military planes, military bases –

JANE. That's what you'd expect.

So the fact that they're not, that suggests to me that they're trying to hide something.

RAY. Really?

JANE. Sometimes, when you want to hide something, you make it look like everything else. And then nobody notices.

RAY. What makes you think it's the CIA?

JANE. They have form on snatching people. And the Americans are very, very keen to stop another 9/11.

RAY. If that is what they're doing, I'm sure there's a good reason.

JANE. Then they won't mind me finding out, will they?

RAY. The situation is pretty scary right now. Whatever they're doing, they probably need to do it.

JANE. You can't have someone snatched off a street in Karachi, and then just disappear.

RAY. These aren't nice people they're dealing with, Jane!

JANE. The CIA aren't nice people, Ray.

RAY. Well, I'm sorry. I don't want to be mixed up in something like this.

JANE. You're not mixed up, Ray. It's nothing whatever to do with you.

RAY. No – sorry. I don't want –

JANE. Don't be a bollocks, Ray! I can find this out from anywhere, I just came to you because –

RAY. It's a delicate situation, you see. They let guys like me stand around at airports and take photos because basically they know we're on their side. We're not going to rock the boat. But it would just take one person to tread on their toes, and that would muck it up for everybody else.

JANE. Don't be stupid, Ray.

RAY. Let the big guys take care of this stuff. We're the little
people, remember.

JANE. Speak for yourself, Ray. I'm not a little person.

RAY. You are to them.

JANE. I can't believe you're talking like this, Ray.

Just print those logs off for me and I'll –

RAY. No. You can't have them.

He shuts down his computer.

JANE. What?

RAY. I'm sorry.

JANE. You're more worried about your plane-spotter pals than
people disappearing?

RAY. The more you hassle me, the more I think I don't want to
have anything to do with this.

JANE. Ray?

RAY. To be honest, it all sounds a bit crazy. I don't quite know
what you think, but it sounds –

JANE. Look, I just want the flight logs.

RAY. Masked men? Disappearing suspects?

JANE. You've got no idea.

RAY. You've always been susceptible to a good conspiracy
theory.

JANE. Fuck off, Ray.

RAY. I'll get you a duvet.

*A door slams in the distance. Footsteps receding. JANE
listens.*

Scene Three

Later that night. JANE, *in an old T-shirt of* RAY's, *is sitting at* RAY's *desk, printing off the flight logs as quietly as possible.*

ANA *appears at the door.*

ANA. What are you doing?

JANE. Oh, Ana – hi! Just back from work?

ANA. I didn't realise you were staying.

JANE. On the sofa.

I'm sorry about earlier, I didn't mean to be…

ANA. What are you doing?

JANE. Oh, just…

Tell me about your blog.

ANA. Are you really interested?

JANE. Sure.

ANA. It's all about the campaign to prevent a war with Iraq. I gather together interesting articles, post information about demos, that kind of thing.

JANE. So are you a journalist or an activist?

ANA. Both, I suppose.

JANE. And Ray's cool with that?

ANA. He's not interested.

JANE. Does he know?

ANA. He doesn't ask.

JANE. He worries.

ANA. He's a dad.

JANE. Yes, so he wants to know about your life. Your
boyfriends…

Maybe you could open up to him a bit more.

ANA. He's just so protective.

JANE. Why is that, do you think?

ANA. I dunno. I think he's got some thing about me being like
Mum. Because she was political, he's scared I will be as well.

JANE. I don't think he realised what he was getting himself in to.

ANA. Did you know my mum?

JANE. I met her. I didn't know her well.

ANA. What was she like?

JANE. Why are you asking me?

ANA. Dad is selective about what he tells me.

JANE. In what way?

ANA. He just tells me the mumsy stuff. Not what she thought.
What she believed in.

JANE. I guess it's hard for him.

ANA. Did you like her?

JANE. Well, you know. Ray goes off to Central America in his
summer holiday and he comes back with this beautiful,
Latino girlfriend. Who's pregnant. It kind of changed things.

ANA. Is there something he isn't telling me, do you think?

JANE. I think he's just still grieving.

ANA. It was a long time ago!

JANE. I know.

ANA. If you find out anything, will you tell me?

JANE *shrugs*. ANA *picks up a printout*.

What's this you're printing?

JANE *takes it off her.*

JANE. Just some stuff for a piece I'm writing. Your dad was helping me.

ANA. He let you go on his computer? Amazing.

JANE. Just some techie stuff.

ANA. Is it to do with planes?

JANE. Yes, sort of.

ANA. He'll be so chuffed. Finally his planes are important.

JANE. Don't mention to him about the printing, though, if you don't mind.

ANA. Why not?

JANE. You know what he's like. Very protective.

ANA. Doesn't he know you're printing these off?

JANE. It's to do with the so-called War on Terror. To be honest, I don't know what Ray's worried about.

ANA. So you thought you'd print these out without telling him.

JANE. He doesn't need to be worried.

ANA. What about honesty and transparency?

JANE. Yes. That's what I'm doing here. People in power need to be called to account.

ANA. I mean between friends.

You've got no right to go into Dad's computer.

JANE. Don't be silly, Ana! Sometimes, when you're a journalist –

ANA. What? You stop respecting your friends' privacy?

JANE. Sometimes the ends justify the means.

ANA. Listen to yourself.

JANE. What?

ANA. Listen to what you're saying.

JANE. Okay. Fine. Why don't you go and wake him up right now and tell him what an outrageous breach of trust I'm committing.

A beat.

ANA. I really want to know more about my mum. He won't talk to me, but he'd tell you. If you ask him for me, I won't mention this to him.

Okay?

ANA *doesn't move.*

After a moment, JANE *shrugs assent and continues printing.*

Scene Four

The sound of a jet taking off, very close, very loud.

A day later. JANE *in her mum's house, with huge bundles of flight-data printouts. She's made a sort of office on the kitchen table, but there's chaos all around. She is struggling to make sense of the data she's got from the website.*

JANE. N829MG. GLF 3. 15 May. 0633. KJNX.

EDDF. 1021. OPKC.

17 May. 0333. EDDF MUGM.

N829MG – that's my plane.

GLF 3 – it's a Gulfstream III.

15 May 6.33 a.m.

KJNX – Johnston County Airport, North Carolina.

Where the hell is that?

EDDF – Frankfurt, Germany.

10.21.

Arrives 10.21

Or leaves 10.21?

So then it goes EDDF OPKC.

Frankfurt, Germany to Karachi, Pakistan.

17th May at 3.33 a.m. OPKC (Karachi) to EDDF (Frankfurt) and 07.34 EDDF (Frankfurt) to MUGM.

MUGM?

She consults her documents.

MUGM – Guantanamo.

JANE *looks up.*

She sees an empty chair. There are jump leads on the chair.

Scene Five

The same night, at RAY*'s house.* ANA *is engrossed in her laptop.* RAY *enters, still in his high-vis vest.*

ANA. Hey, Dad. There's a baked potato for you, if you want.

RAY. You little angel – I'm starving. Thanks, sweetie.

ANA. That was a late one.

RAY. Just a puncture. But the spare was punctured too, so I had to tow her. Poor woman was waiting for me on the side of the A449 near Stourbridge for an hour and a half, with a three-year-old.

ANA. She must have been pleased to see you.

RAY. Then I came home via the airfield.

ANA. At this time of night!

RAY. Pete had tipped me off there was something interesting coming in.

It was fascinating, actually, it was –

ANA *mimes falling instantly asleep and waking with a start.*

ANA. Oh sorry, I think I nodded off.

RAY. What've you been up to? How's your assignment?

ANA. It's fine. Dad?

RAY. Yeah?

ANA. What happened, exactly, the other night?

RAY. When?

ANA. With Jane.

RAY. With Jane? Nothing happened.

ANA. She was wearing your T-shirt.

RAY. She didn't have any pyjamas with her.

ANA. Is she an old flame?

RAY. We just go back a long way.

ANA. Is she a potential new flame?

RAY. Ana, don't be daft!

ANA. Phew. You had me worried there.

RAY. What you have to understand about Jane, sweetie, is –

I know she can be a bit abrasive. But that's just a front.

ANA. Underneath she's a really beautiful person?

RAY. She had a very hard time of it.

Her mum –

She was on her own, and in a bit of a mess.

As it went on it got worse.

She was a drinker, the mum, and –

It was all very bad.

We did everything we could. Jane knew she could always come to us to escape. At one point she was virtually living with us.

I'm a bit like her big brother.

And she's a very respected journalist now, so I thought she'd be a useful contact.

ANA. Well, either way – don't get your hopes up.

RAY. Point taken.

ANA. I thought I might invite Sam down here. To meet you.

RAY. Oh, great – yeah. Sam, he's your…? Yes, do.

ANA. Okay.

RAY. Is it… serious, then?

    ANA *shrugs*.

ANA. I dunno. But I think you'll like him.

RAY. Great! That's –

Good. I'll try not to be too embarrassing.

ANA. Yeah. But don't try *too* hard, or that might be embarrassing.

RAY. Oh, shut up, you.

    They laugh.

ANA. You had me a bit worried about Jane, you know.

RAY. I'm sorry about that.

ANA. But maybe you should, you know…

Not with Jane, but –

RAY. What?

ANA. Maybe it's time for you to 'move on'?

He sighs.

I won't be embarrassing, if you want to bring a girlfriend home.

He laughs.

RAY. Yeah, I know. I suppose I just haven't, you know – met anyone. Yet.

ANA. All those grateful women you pick up by the roadside?

RAY. Ana!

ANA. Sam went to Central America for his gap year.

RAY. Did he?

ANA. It's a shame…

Silence.

He was asking me all these questions, about Mum.

RAY. About what?

ANA. About her.

RAY. What did you tell him?

ANA. All the stories. How you met in San Salvador. How she took supplies to the rebels in her father's government car. The time you drove to the coast and drank fresh coconuts with a straw and slept in hammocks on the beach. I know all that stuff.

RAY. So…?

ANA. Why aren't we in touch with Mum's family in El Salvador?

RAY. Your grandma sends you birthday cards.

ANA. Yeah, but…

RAY. They weren't too pleased when your mum got pregnant with you. Then I took her away to Europe. And they thought it was me who got her into helping the FMLN.

ANA. But why didn't they come over when she got sick?

RAY. She didn't really want to see them, to be honest.

ANA. But she knew she had cancer, surely she –

RAY. We didn't know it was –

We didn't know she was going to –

It was a difficult time.

ANA. That's what you always say.

RAY. It was, Ana. What more can I say?

Silence.

ANA. Are there any photos, or letters from that time? Or... anything?

RAY. What's brought this on, sweetie?

ANA. Was she politically involved over here?

RAY. No. She wasn't.

ANA. Really? She must have been!

RAY. You were only a baby, she had other things on her mind.

ANA. I just can't picture it, picture her – at that time.

RAY. She was a young mum, like any young mum...

ANA. I just always feel there's something you're not –

RAY. Sweetie, I'm sorry. I'm tired. It's late.

ANA. She's my mother, and I just want to know –

RAY. There's nothing to know, Ana.

I'm done in.

Thanks for the potato.

Scene Six

Mid-January. The sound of rapid breathing. It could be fear, or pain. In the shadows, a figure waits. A jet goes past, very loud.

JANE. Okay, here we go. N829MG.

She looks up something on the screen.

Owned by Paramount Executive, based in Johnston County, North Carolina.

Okay. Alright. That's it – Johnston County, North Carolina.

Chief Executive of Paramount Executive: Yes!

Michael Holmes.

Search: Michael Holmes.

Another jet screams past. JANE listens. She hears nothing.

Right.

Holmes, Michael. Date of birth 1954. Current address?

Nothing. Previous address?

Nothing.

Business or corporate records?

Not a dicky bird.

Social Security number… Blah blah.

Social Security number issued: 2001. October.

Huh? That's strange.

Why didn't you have a social security number until you were forty-seven, Michael Holmes?

Until just after 9/11?

Her mobile rings. She jumps. Answers it.

Jane Simonds.

It's her old newspaper editor. She bristles.

Hi, Jasper. If you're ringing to offer me my old job back, the answer's no.

It's a big story, Jas. I'm not going to rush it.

Yeah, yeah, Pulitzer-Schmulitzer.

What is it?

Oh Christ, Jasper, don't insult me. I don't do that kind of crap, that's why I –

No.

I'm not that desperate.

No. Sorry.

But, Jas, would you do one favour for me?

I need to make a phone call, and I don't want to do it from anywhere they can trace me.

Can I come into the office? It'll just take half an hour.

Bright lights dazzle the stage. JANE *is caught in the lights.*

RAY *enters with takeaway. The lights fade.*

Scene Seven

*Late January. JANE, in her mother's house. There are half-
packed boxes and half-full bin liners everywhere. JANE is
working on her laptop, papers strewn around. RAY is trying to
clear enough space on the table to set out the takeaway he's
brought.*

JANE. My plane…

RAY. You still like lamb ghosh?

JANE. It doesn't have a regular schedule, but I've tracked it –

RAY. I got a chicken tikka masala as well, just in case.

JANE. Cairo. Damascus. Amman, Jordan.

RAY. Are the plates still in this cupboard here? Yes! Nothing's
   changed.

   Lamb or chicken, Jane?

JANE. Yeah, thanks – whatever.

   RAY is rummaging in a drawer.

RAY. Knives and forks?… Here they are.

JANE. What's the key thing that links these destinations?

RAY. I dunno. Nice climate? Can I move these papers?

   He picks up the flight-log printouts.

JANE. Come on, Ray! These are all nasty, repressive regimes
   with appalling human-rights records where –

RAY. Where did you get these from?

JANE. What?

RAY. These are from my computer, Jane. I told you not to.

JANE. Ah, yes. I was going to tell you…

RAY. What the fuck, Jane?

JANE. Sorry, Ray. But they were sitting there, and –

RAY. But I told you –

JANE. I could've got them anyway, Ray.

The point is, these are regimes where torture is endemic. And – this is the key – all close allies of the US. So if they want to use 'enhanced' interrogation techniques on their terror suspects, if they want to torture them, basically, but they need to be able to deny they're doing it, that's what they do.

Outsource.

Outsource torture.

RAY. Jane –

JANE. It's ingenious. You've got to hand it to them. Talk about blue-sky thinking. You've got deniability, plus 'international cooperation'.

RAY. First of all, you had no right.

JANE. Don't be such a little Nimby, Ray! Who cares about your sodding printouts, compared to people being kept in secret prisons?

RAY. I just don't get what makes you think that the CIA are involved in this.

JANE. Think? I know. I phoned the company that owns the plane.

I asked to charter the plane, N829MG.

They said it was one of their planes, but it wasn't available for private hire. I asked if I had to go through the US Government to hire it.

They said they couldn't tell me, but they'd get someone to call me back.

Within fifteen minutes, they called back.

Listen.

Listen to this:

She plays back the recorded phone conversation on her digital recorder.

JANE'S VOICE. Hello?

AMERICAN VOICE. Hello. I am calling because you have been in contact with a US company regarding a certain plane.

JANE'S VOICE. Who am I speaking to?

AMERICAN VOICE. Do you work for a government authority?

JANE'S VOICE. Why do you ask?

AMERICAN VOICE. You're calling from a number in the UK. Are you from a UK government authority?

JANE'S VOICE. Do I have to be?

AMERICAN VOICE. Can you confirm your security clearance, please?

JANE switches off the digital recorder.

RAY is visibly shaken.

RAY. Shit.

JANE. You see?

What do you think?

RAY. You didn't call from your own phone, did you?

JANE. Of course not. I used the newspaper office.

RAY. What if they track you?

JANE. I've got them!

RAY. They're the CIA. They can do what they want anyway.

JANE. So why do you think they're going to all that trouble to disguise what they're doing?

Deniability.

They don't want the world to find out that they are unlawfully detaining and torturing terror suspects.

Because not even the CIA can do that.

RAY. But how can you prove it? Even if the plane is being used by the CIA, you can't prove what it's being used for.

JANE. I'm getting closer, Ray. I'm getting closer.

RAY. Look, Jane. Just come and eat your takeaway.

Let's spend an evening together.

This is all a bit bonkers, it's taking over your life.

JANE. If I can break this story, Ray…

RAY. You're living here in chaos, you're sneaking on to my computer…

JANE. Don't you see?

RAY. Ana's back at uni, so I've got a bit more time, I'd be happy to –

JANE. Don't you see what it would mean?

RAY. What?

JANE. If I can prove that the CIA are kidnapping suspects without trials, without due process –

RAY. Yes, but how? How are you going to prove it?

JANE. Oh, shut up, Ray.

I don't know, do I?

I don't fucking well know.

JANE *sees an upturned chair. The crackle of electricity. A flash of electric light. Another crackle.*

Scene Eight

*Early morning, 15 February 2003. ANA and RAY at home.
ANA is wrapped up warm for the 'Stop the War' demo. She's
made a placard saying 'NOT IN MY NAME'.*

ANA. Come on, Dad – come with me.

RAY. It's such a hassle, getting to London.

It's freezing weather. It's probably going to snow…

ANA. Don't be so provincial. When was the last time you were
in London?

RAY. Look, you're supposed to be home for the week on study
leave. You're not supposed to be running back to London for
a demo!

ANA. Sam'll be there. You want to meet Sam, don't you?

RAY. I thought you were going to bring him home to meet me.

ANA. Oh, for God's sake, Dad! It's about Iraq. Do you think
we should invade? Do you really think they have WMD that
can reach us –

RAY. No. I don't. But I think Saddam Hussein is a nasty piece
of work.

ANA. Oh, so what about Burma? What about North Korea? Do
you think we should invade them, too?

RAY. You know I don't want a war, but I do think that the
government are privy to information we don't know about
and you've got to trust that –

ANA. If that's so, they need a UN Security Council resolution.
Right?

RAY. Right.

ANA. Have you heard of Katharine Gun?

RAY. Who?

ANA. She worked at GCHQ and she found out that the US were trying to run illegal taps on the UN Security Council members to get dirt on them so that they could use it to pressure them into voting for their war.

RAY. Be that as it may –

ANA. No, Dad – that's an outrage! And as a whistle-blower she is now facing a prison sentence, when all she did was expose –

RAY. Exactly! Don't get mixed up in these kind of things, Ana. They're bigger than us.

ANA. I'm just talking about going on a peaceful demonstration.

RAY. I've been on plenty of demos. There are all kinds of people who want to hijack events like this, things can turn nasty…

ANA. Dad! Dad! How did you become so apathetic?

RAY. I'm not apathetic.

ANA. Demonstrating is your democratic right.

RAY. All kinds of people have lost their lives exercising their democratic rights –

ANA. Do you really think my life is in danger if I go on this demo?

RAY. No. But –

ANA. This is England, Dad. This is 2003.

Scene Nine

JANE *enters with a cup of tea. Her chair isn't where she thought she left it. She's momentarily confused. She sits down, starts wading blearily through her printouts on her laptop.*

JANE. KIAD – Washington DC.

MUGM – Guantanamo, Cuba.

HECA – Amman, Jordan.

No – wait.

She furiously leafs through the papers, checks against something on the screen.

Okay. HECA – Cairo, Egypt.

So. Washington, KIAD.

MUGM, Guantanamo, Cuba.

HECA – that's…

Shit, what is HECA?

She rifles through her papers, searching for one particular piece. All the paper falls on the floor in a big mess. She kneels to pick the papers up. But she just kneels on the floor, defeated.

She hears a helicopter outside her window. The noise gets louder and louder. Suddenly fearful, she goes cautiously to the window and peers out.

Her phone rings. She jumps. Gets a grip. Answers it.

Hi, Jas. What's up?

No – I'm fine.

Go on then – what's your lead?

She listens, interested now.

Wow. Yes – that is good.

Thank you, Jas.

Give me the wife's address then.

She puts down the phone. This is a big break for her. The story is hot again.

Halle-fucking-lujah.

Scene Ten

Mid-March, 2003. At MINA's house.

JANE. Your husband has been missing for a year?

MINA. Yes.

JANE. He left in February last year?

MINA. Yes.

JANE. Which flight was he on?

MINA. I don't think it's going to help.

JANE. Yes. Really. It's important.

MINA. I don't think it's going to help, Miss – what's your name again?

JANE. My name's Jane. I'm an investigative reporter. And I know it must be hard for you, but I have been working on this for some time, and I think I can help you.

MINA *consults her diary.*

MINA. It was the 24th February, Pakistan International flight 639 at 16.50.

JANE. Great. Thank you. Have you heard from him at all?

MINA. I haven't. No.

JANE. He hasn't phoned, or texted, or emailed?

MINA. No.

JANE. And have you had any other news of him? From anyone?

MINA. I've been through all this already. With the police.

JANE. I'm not police. I may be able to help you.

MINA. I don't think so.

JANE. Have the security services contacted you at all?

MINA. Are you kidding?

JANE. Were you contacted by any... officers? Military personnel? Anybody like that been in touch, asking questions?

MINA. I don't know what you think, but you're wasting your time.

JANE. Since your husband went, disappeared – have you had any unexplained break-ins? Burglaries?

MINA. Listen, I think you've got the wrong –

What d'you mean, burglaries?

JANE. Have you been broken into?

MINA. Yes.

JANE. Uh-huh. Did they take anything?

MINA. …No.

JANE. Did they take anything of your husband's?

MINA. No.

JANE. Like a phone, or a laptop?

MINA. What exactly are you getting at?

JANE. They didn't take any cash, laptops, jewellery? That's a bit unusual, isn't it?

Mrs Ahmed, what do you think has happened to your husband?

MINA. I know exactly what's happened to him.

JANE. Really?

MINA. He's left me. He's gone off with another woman.

JANE. I'm sorry?

MINA. Just before he left, I found out that he was having an affair.

JANE. An affair?

MINA. He denied it. But he was.

Silence.

She was out in Pakistan. He's gone to be with her. He can't face telling me, and having the arguments, so he's just gone. Without a word.

JANE. No. I don't think so.

MINA. I know he was having an affair. I know he was lying to me.

JANE. Mrs Ahmed –

MINA. Can you imagine what it's like for me? That he couldn't even tell me!

JANE. I'm sorry. This is… This isn't quite what I was expecting.

MINA. What am I supposed to tell the kids?

If he tries to get the kids off me, and take them over there, then I can tell you, he'll have a fight on his hands.

JANE. I don't think that's what's happened to him.

MINA. And his family are colluding. I phoned them, obviously.
When he didn't return home. They said this kind of thing
happens, there. They said people go missing sometimes.

I know they're covering for him. They never accepted me.

JANE. Did you ask them about this?

MINA. They deny it, of course. But I *know* he was having an
affair.

JANE. I believe that he was kidnapped.

MINA. Yes, that's what his family says. So why hasn't anyone
asked for a ransom?

JANE. No, I mean, kidnapped by the CIA. And transported to a
prison in Jordan for interrogation.

A beat.

MINA. You are joking, aren't you?

JANE. My newspaper has been in contact with a Moroccan man
who has been released from a jail in Jordan. He said there was
a British guy in the cell next to him, called Amin Ahmed.

That's your husband, isn't it?

MINA. But –

JANE. I know this must come as a shock, but –

MINA *laughs.*

MINA. Amin isn't a terrorist.

JANE. Did he have radical leanings? A renewed interest in
Islam? Some dodgy new friends, maybe?

MINA. Look. Here's a photo of me and Amin at our wedding.

Where's an album…

She gets a photo album out.

There he is, when our oldest son was born.

JANE. Yes. Of course…

MINA. He's a Villa supporter.

Look. Here he is taking our older son to Dudley Zoo.

JANE. I understand that it's very hard for you to comprehend –

Just give me a minute to –

JANE *gets her laptop out.*

MINA. Comprehend? You know, you're completely mad. In the last few months I have wondered if I've gone mad myself. But *you*, you are absolutely barking, raving mad.

Scene Eleven

RAY, *in his high-vis vest, takes a call on his mobile phone.*

Scene Twelve

MINA *and* JANE *at* MINA*'s house.*

JANE. Let me show you something. Please, Mrs Ahmed.

I'm not trying to make your life difficult, but I think I can offer an explanation…

She's scrolling around on the laptop, trying to find the flight logs.

I can show you the flight logs of all the planes for February last year. We could find the plane that I believe transported your husband from Islamabad to Amman.

MINA. You can show me all the flight logs you like. I just don't believe that Amin has been kidnapped by the CIA.

JANE *is still searching for the flight log.*

JANE. You said you thought he was having an affair. Was there anything unusual in his behaviour...?

MINA. I know he was having an affair.

JANE. Perhaps he was being secretive for other reasons. Did you have proof?

MINA. Yes.

JANE. What proof?

MINA. I looked at his emails.

JANE *stops looking at the flight logs.*

JANE. Oh. I see.

MINA. She's barely been out of the village, but apparently she can use email.

JANE. And you confronted him?

MINA. No. I didn't.

JANE. Why not?

MINA. I couldn't admit I'd been looking through his emails!

JANE. You see, it might be – and I'm not saying this is the case – but those emails might have been in code. Or the security services might have thought they were in code.

MINA. What?!

JANE. Was there anything else in his emails? Anything else that might explain... or be a cause for concern...?

MINA. No.

JANE. Nothing?

MINA. Nothing at all.

JANE. If only you still had his laptop.

MINA. I have.

JANE. What!

MINA. He didn't take it with him.

JANE. Why not?

MINA. What d'you mean, why not?

JANE. Surely he would have taken his laptop...?

MINA. I...

A beat.

I...

JANE. What?

MINA. I was so angry, you see – when I found the emails.

I tried to talk to him. But he just kept denying everything. I just had to be sure. So I took his laptop out of his packing and then...

I wasn't thinking clearly.

JANE. You...?

MINA. Yes. And then I hid it at the salon where I work.

JANE. Where is it now?

MINA. Here.

JANE. In this room?

MINA. In the cupboard. I haven't touched it since.

MINA *produces the laptop. She turns it on.*

JANE. Can I have a look?

MINA. Why?

JANE. There might be something...

MINA. No. It's personal.

JANE. Don't worry, I'm only interested in –

MINA. No. You can't.

JANE. Mrs Ahmed, if I could just –

MINA. No. I'm sorry.

JANE. Anyway, that's why they broke in. You said there was a burglary?

MINA. Yes.

JANE. They were trying to get hold of his laptop. But you managed to keep it away from them.

MINA. I just didn't want the kids to find it.

JANE. I understand.

Do you think I could have that glass of water after all?

MINA. Sure.

MINA exits. JANE waits till she's out of the room. She looks at the laptop. She waits. She can't bear it.

She picks up the laptop, opens it then thinks better of it. Closes it. But it's still on her lap when MINA *appears with the glass of water.*

What the hell are you doing?

JANE. Sorry.

I just need –

If you would just allow me to have a look at the browsing history.

MINA. I told you not to –

JANE. And I respect that.

I didn't look.

But, Mrs Ahmed, Mina, please.

This could prove that your husband didn't leave you at all.
Do you see? It may be that he can't get in touch, rather than
he's choosing not to.

MINA *opens the laptop, gives it to* JANE.

JANE *starts scrolling through his browsing history.*

Ah!

MINA. What?

JANE. 'Live from Gaza' blogspot. Hamas discussion forum.

MINA. There's nothing extremist about being interested in
Palestine.

JANE. Here, look at this.

Chechnya. Bosnia...

MINA. Martyrs videos?

Look – it doesn't mean...

JANE. And there's more. Look.

MINA. But he's just looking. Maybe he was just trying to find
out, we don't get the full story here, you know – it's not until
you start looking at the Arabic TV stations...

JANE. Look at this, here. A forum. He's been quite chatty.

MINA. I didn't think he...

She reads.

JANE. Quite colourfully chatty. That in itself is enough to get
him on the list.

MINA. What list?

JANE. All these kind of websites are monitored.

MINA. This is crazy. I don't believe this.

JANE. Half the people on these forums are informers. They
strike up conversations, win people's trust – then shop them.
For cash.

MINA. I don't believe any of this.

JANE. What don't you believe?

MINA. Any of it. Amin's not a jihadi. He's other things, but not that. Look at these emails, to Aafia.

JANE. I'm not saying he is a jihadi, but in the current climate, it doesn't look good – does it?

MINA. Amin was lying to me. Lying through his teeth. But he wasn't –

JANE. Would he really just disappear like that, and not even try and contact his kids?

Silence.

This is just the beginning, Mina. We're just scratching the surface, here. You wait. This is down-the-rabbit-hole territory. This is through-the-looking-glass land.

Only it's real.

Scene Thirteen

RAY *at the perimeter fence. He checks the photo he's just taken on the back of his digital camera. He's amazed by what he's got.*

Scene Fourteen

JANE *at* MINA*'s.* MINA *is looking through Amin's laptop.*
JANE *is finding the plane-spotting websites on her own laptop.*

MINA. I can't believe what I'm seeing here.

JANE. I'm going through all the flight logs of the day Amin
disappeared, and the following day.

Here we go.

This here – see – this is the plane he was booked onto.
Pakistan International flight 639.

Here it is, leaving at 16.50. And arriving at Islamabad.

Now I'm going to search for any planes leaving Islamabad
going to Jordan around the same time –

Here's one leaving forty-five minutes later.

Oh wow. The tail number...

This is my plane. I know this plane.

MINA *looks at the screen but it's all just numbers and letters
to her.*

MINA. I had no idea he was looking at this kind of stuff. Who
is this person who's sending him all these links? I've never
heard of him.

JANE. This is the one.

I have confirmed that this is a CIA-operated plane.

JANE *is still searching on her laptop.* MINA *goes back to
Amin's laptop.*

MINA. It's horrible. It's...

There's footage of a woman being stoned to death.

JANE *looks at* MINA. *She stops searching and gets her digital recorder out.*

JANE. Mrs Ahmed, do you mind if I start recording our conversation?

MINA. Call me Mina. But don't record anything.

Please.

Jane, what should I do?

JANE. My article will throw light on the case. I give you my word that I will respect your...

MINA. Why would I want to throw light on what's happened?

JANE. This story needs to be told.

MINA. I don't want everyone to know!

JANE. People will be outraged. You can start a campaign.

MINA. What do you mean?

JANE. To get him released, Mrs Ahmed. Mina.

MINA. Released?

JANE. Questions need to be asked. As he's a British citizen, either the Government must help you, or they're implicated, in which case –

MINA. No, I mean, what should I do if he's guilty?

JANE. Guilty? That's not really the issue here.

MINA. How can it not be the issue?

JANE. Mina, regardless of what he's done, he's still entitled to be treated according to the rule of law. He still has human rights.

MINA. What if he had been radicalised? What if he was planning to murder people? He was having an affair, but now he thinks that adulteresses should be stoned?

JANE. Looking at radical websites isn't the same as bombing people.

MINA. I don't know who he is any more.

You can't record any of this.

JANE *gets the wedding photo*.

JANE. He's your husband. He's the same person.

MINA. I'm sorry you won't get your scoop.

JANE. I'm not here for a scoop!

MINA. Of course you are. What else are you here for?

I think you should go now.

JANE. What if he is innocent, Mina?

MINA *breaks down*.

MINA. I don't know what to think.

I don't know what to believe.

I've got him denying he's fallen in love with someone else, when I know he has.

I've got you saying the CIA have got him.

It's all mad.

I've just got used to the fact that he's gone.

I've handled the business, I've paid the mortgage, I've dealt with everything.

What was I supposed to tell the kids? I told them the truth. What I thought was the truth.

But now, if I have to –

Now what am I going to tell them? What'll it do to them?

I don't want to! I just don't want to.

JANE. Please, Mina. Talk to me. You deserve to have a voice in all this.

MINA. I don't want a voice! I just want to get on with my life.

You do what you want.

JANE. All I can do is write about it. That's how I can help. I can get people to take notice.

MINA. And how does that help me?

What's it going to do to my boys?

JANE. Look at these flight logs. Please. I think if you see that, you'll begin to understand.

JANE *goes back to the laptop. As she's talking, she's doing the internet search.*

What I've got is this particular plane, which I have proved is a CIA plane. I know its tail number. So if I refresh the search, it will come up that this plane was at Islamabad airport on 25 February, at the time that your husband arrived there, and that it took off forty-five minutes later bound for Amman, Jordan.

Why isn't it…?

It's glitching.

Let me try again. I did this search just now and it showed up, quite clearly –

MINA. It's not coming up. You must have made a mistake.

JANE. Hang on.

I did it just now.

Shit.

MINA. 'Error: No data available.' That's your proof, is it? That's the thing that's going to start to make sense of all this?

JANE. God. It's disappeared from the flight logs. It was here, just now.

I saw it.

She looks at MINA.

You don't believe me, do you?

MINA. I think you'd better go.

Scene Fifteen

End of March, 2003. RAY *and* JANE *are back at* RAY*'s, eating a meal.* ANA *is there for the Easter holidays.*

JANE. I have an eyewitness account that a British citizen is being held in a Jordanian jail.

I've got a mystery plane I've proved is operated by the CIA.

I know it visits the torture capitals of the world.

I've even got a flight plan of a private jet which went from Islamabad to Jordan the day the UK citizen went missing.

ANA. Fucking hell.

JANE. But the wife is in complete denial. She doesn't believe me and she won't cooperate.

And now –

ANA. This is incredible.

JANE. ... now, Ray – are you listening?

RAY. I've got you both an early Easter egg for pudding.

ANA. Can I help you? If you need a researcher, or –

JANE. What? No, it's okay thanks, Ana.

Wait till you hear this.

My plane, Ray, has disappeared from the flight logs.

No trace of it.

I saw it, it was there.

Now it's gone.

ANA. Oh, Jesus.

RAY. Maybe they've stopped using it, then.

JANE. It's disappeared retrospectively.

ANA. Shit. That's so creepy.

JANE. They know I'm on to them.

Thanks for this, Ray. I love dark chocolate.

RAY. I know.

ANA *clocks this*.

ANA. Yes, thanks, Dad. Sorry I didn't...

Have some of mine.

JANE. Maybe it was the phone call. Maybe they're watching Mrs Ahmed.

Or it could be the websites I've been using are monitored...

RAY. Jane. Perhaps you should drop this story.

ANA. Of course she shouldn't drop it!

JANE. I know I'm right, Ray. I know it's happening.

But nobody believes me. Not even you.

ANA. I believe you.

RAY. I know this is very important to you. But if the evidence isn't there...

JANE. The evidence *is* there. I just can't see it.

RAY. Aren't you going to be late for work?

ANA. I'm going. I'm just saying...

JANE. Thanks, Ana. Thanks for your support.

ANA. Anyway, Jane, I'm serious, about –

You wouldn't have to pay me.

JANE. You're sweet. Thanks.

RAY. Go on, you'll be late.

ANA. Okay. I'm going.

She goes.

JANE. You think I'm losing it, don't you, Ray?

RAY. No. I think you're quite stressed, and –

JANE. You don't believe me, about the plane disappearing?

RAY. I don't know. I think you're a bit obsessed, and there could be a perfectly simple explanation.

JANE. Christ, Ray.

RAY. You've been working too hard, you've been staying up, night after night.

And I think you're more upset than you're acknowledging, about your mother.

JANE. My mother?

RAY. It must be bringing up all kinds of memories, clearing out that house.

JANE. Thank Christ for that Home, Ray.

She wanders. She gets abusive. They have to keep her locked up.

It's a prison, effectively.

RAY. I'm sorry.

JANE. I couldn't cope with her, Ray. I couldn't care for her.

RAY. She's an old lady.

JANE. Don't you remember what she was like with me, when I was a kid? Don't you remember?

I used to think, Ray's mum won't let this carry on, she'll do something, she'll tell someone.

RAY. I don't think we really realised…

JANE. You never believed me about the diaries, did you?

RAY. What diaries?

JANE. When my mum found my secret diaries, she didn't like what she read in them, so she burned them.

RAY. What was in them?

JANE. That I hated her, basically.

RAY. Jane.

JANE. So she burned them. And she tried to lock me in my room. That was the night that I ran all the way to your house, and your mum took me in.

Then, in the morning, your mum sent me back home.

RAY. I didn't realise she burned your diaries.

JANE. I told you she did! After that, she used to search my bedroom. That's why I hid them in the pig shed.

RAY. I thought you were being paranoid.

JANE. I wasn't being paranoid then. I'm not being paranoid now.

Why won't you believe me?

If they can disappear a person, Ray, then disappearing a plane from the flight logs is easy.

RAY. Is there any chance you've got it wrong?

JANE. You of all people, Ray.

Pause.

Does Ana think we…?

Silence.

Remember our teenage escapades in the woods at night. Remember that holly bush that had grown over, like a tunnel? You used to dare me to run through it.

RAY. Yes.

It's not the time to be poking about in a story like this.

We're at war with Iraq, and America is our ally…

JANE. And?

RAY. Certain things –

JANE. Are justified?

RAY. Even if you're right, and I'm not saying that you are, there are terrorists out there and somebody's got to deal with them.

I just don't want you to get hurt.

JANE. In your mind I'm still the poor little girl from down the lane who has to be looked out for.

He laughs.

You don't have to protect me, Ray. I'm not that little girl any more.

RAY. Yeah you are.

A beat.

And I'm still the one you turn to. Which I take as a backhanded kind of a compliment.

A pause.

JANE. I found a Nicaragua Solidarity Campaign badge you gave me, that summer. You pinned it on to my T-shirt.

RAY *laughs. Sighs.*

You used to meet me when I'd finished my shift at The Plough and we'd walk back across the fields.

RAY. I know.

JANE. Remember that abandoned caravan? We used to break in.

RAY. I don't think it was really abandoned. It was just parked.

JANE. And then we had our little –

RAY. Our fling?

JANE. Our summer of love.

Give it its proper due.

You know a funny thing, Ray? I hope you don't mind me saying this. But I think you should know.

RAY. What's that then?

JANE. It was brief but I can honestly say that was some of the most gorgeous sex I've ever had.

A beat.

Sorry. I thought you should know.

A pause.

I still think about it.

The tenderness.

He thinks she's going to kiss him. He's not sure what he'll do if she does.

I'm not being paranoid about this story, Ray.

Do you believe me?

Silence.

Fucking hell. You don't.

She pulls away from him. The moment is gone.

Scene Sixteen

The next day. JANE working in her mother's house. She can't make sense of anything.

She keeps seeing scenes of violence and torture which aren't there. The radio is on – more reports of the Allied advance on Baghdad.

She flicks through her notebooks, and comes across the paper napkin that ANA wrote down the name of her blog on. JANE looks up the blog.

Scene Seventeen

Later that day. The pub garden of The Plough. ANA is engrossed in her laptop. JANE approaches.

ANA. Hiya! What're you doing here?

JANE. I looked at your blog and I saw my story.

ANA. Oh. Well – sorry.

JANE. Even as a student you have to understand something about professional integrity.

ANA. So why haven't you published it? You're just sitting on it and doing nothing –

JANE. Because I haven't got all the information yet.

ANA. You know it's happening. You've got the flight logs – you can show where those planes are going...

JANE. I can't – yet – prove that those planes are doing anything untoward. They could just be transporting diplomats.

ANA. It's pretty obvious, though. Publish the logs, and get the CIA to deny it.

JANE. If those flight logs are in the public domain, it weakens the credibility of the detainees.

ANA. Why?

JANE. If detainees are released, they will give statements about where they think they were taken, on what dates. Then I can use the flight logs to verify their stories.

ANA. Okay, but –

JANE. But if they are already in the public domain, the CIA lawyers can argue that they're just pegging their story to the existing flight plans.

ANA. Okay. If you say so.

JANE. I have got twenty years' experience of this kind of thing.

You've got to take it off your blog.

ANA. It's your story, and you want to control it. Fair enough.

But I still think people need to know about this story.

JANE. Who's going to read it on your blog? A couple of your student friends?

ANA. It's a global network, and if, for example, we decide to start an online petition –

JANE. Oh. Great. That'll really help.

ANA. The 'Stop the War' online campaign got a million people to demonstrate.

JANE. And did that stop the war?

ANA. So when are *you* going to publish the story? Why are you even doing this story?

JANE. I'm a journalist.

I understand about how news works.

And I have to wait until the right moment to publish.

ANA. I'd say now is the right moment. Right now, when people are being tortured in secret prisons...

JANE. Now is not the right time. Now, people are worried about the war. They're worried about terrorist attacks in the UK. They aren't worried about whether some suspected terrorists are being tortured by the CIA.

ANA. They would be if they knew!

JANE. Last year, the *Washington Post* published a story about a man who was bundled onto a plane by masked men in Pakistan. There was a similar story in Italy. What happened when those articles were published?

Nothing.

ANA. The problem is with the mainstream press. But there are other options and I'm not going to sit here and know that's going on and not *do* something about it!

JANE. You're young, Ana.

ANA. Oh, piss off.

ANA moves away.

JANE. Ana! I'm sorry – Ana! Come back.

I didn't mean to patronise you.

ANA stops.

ANA. You've done nothing but patronise me ever since you arrived.

Silence.

JANE. Look. We don't need petitions. We need Government inquiries. I want George Bush and Dick Cheney and Donald Rumsfeld to be in front of a commission answering questions.

ANA. What about stopping torture of prisoners?

JANE. Yes, of course – it's wrong and it doesn't work.

ANA. What d'you mean, 'it doesn't work'?

JANE. Information gained under torture is not admissible in a court of law. Meaning some guy could be guilty as hell, but if you can't use the evidence, he'll walk free.

With a genuine grievance. So then – bingo! You've just radicalised a whole community.

ANA. And if they changed the law, so that evidence from torture was admissible in a court – you'd be okay with that, would you?

JANE. No. Because if you torture people they give you bad information. They say anything to stop the pain. And then you waste resources following up on false leads.

ANA. God you're so cynical.

JANE. No. I'm rigorous. And I can see the big picture.

Ana, I don't want the Taliban to win.

ANA. The Taliban was born in the torture cells of Cairo where the pro-Western, US-backed government was trying to impose their –

JANE. Ana, I *wrote* that article you're quoting.

ANA. Okay. I'm sorry, alright? I just want to do something.

JANE. I know. So do I. Take it down.

Scene Eighteen

A man's suit is being cut in to neat squares. The pieces are being put into a black bin-liner. Sound of distant voices, air-traffic controllers, distorted by static.

That evening. ANA is sitting and looking at RAY's computer. There is a photo on the screen of a small jet.

RAY *enters.*

RAY. What're you doing, Ana?

She turns to face him.

ANA. You're a dark horse, aren't you? Turns out you know a bit more about all this than you were letting on.

RAY. Please close that down. It's private.

ANA. She'd kill to get hold of this picture.

RAY. You've no right, Ana. We have an agreement. I don't snoop in your laptop –

ANA. This is her plane, isn't it? How did you get this picture?

RAY. This is a breach of trust. This is –

ANA. I was just trying to find photos of Mum.

RAY. That's not true. Tell me the truth.

ANA. I just happened to…

RAY. What were you doing in my computer?

Did she put you up to this?

ANA. No! It's for me. This is the kind of thing I write about. This is what I'm interested in.

RAY. In your blog?

ANA. Yes, my blog. If you ever bothered to read it, you'd know that.

It's a political blog, Dad. I gather stories I find on the internet. Eyewitness accounts of events. Whistle-blowers.

RAY. I didn't realise…

ANA. I know. You didn't bother to read it.

RAY. Why didn't you tell me? Why didn't you talk to me about it?

ANA. You'd try and stop me. You didn't even want me to join the 'Stop the War' demo. It's just easier not to tell you.

RAY. Ana…

ANA. I wasn't hiding anything. It was there for you to see, if you wanted to.

RAY. You shouldn't get involved in this kind of thing.

ANA. Why not?

RAY. What we're dealing with is the US security services! In my limited experience with them, I know that you absolutely, Ana, do not mess with them.

ANA. How? Why? What is your experience of them?

RAY. I just know.

Ana, don't ever go into my computer again. And just for once, for once, do what your father tells you.

ANA. Just like that.

RAY. Yes!

ANA. Just shut up and do as you're told.

RAY. This time, yes.

ANA. I don't know what's wrong with you, Dad. Do you think you can just stay neutral? Beyond a point, Dad, that means you aren't just being neutral. You're being complicit.

RAY. Ana –

ANA. And I think you've gone past that point.

I'm embarrassed by you.

I think if Mum was here she'd be embarrassed.

You're betraying everything she was. Everything she stood for.

You're okay. You live in a country where these things don't happen.

But if we just keep turning a blind eye, we'll let all that just slip through our fingers.

Don't you realise that?

What happened to you? How did you become this pathetic creature?

You make me ashamed.

RAY. Ana.

She leaves.

Ana!

Ana!

She's gone.

Scene Nineteen

The sound of scrubbing.

The next day. JANE *at work at her mother's house. She is shoving the contents of a drawer ruthlessly into a black bin bag: old bills, tea towels, knives and forks, old photos, trinkets.*

She stops. She retrieves a childishly made clay bowl decorated with flowers out of the bin bag.

She looks at it.

She puts it back in the bin bag.

She carries on.

She retrieves the pot out of the bin bag again.

RAY *enters.*

JANE. God. What are you doing here?

RAY. I thought I ought to help you.

JANE. Wow – there's an offer. You crazy, romantic fool.

RAY. It's got to be done.

   What shall I do?

JANE. Don't bother.

RAY. Shall I make up some more of these boxes?

   RAY *makes up some flat-packed cardboard boxes. They work in stony silence.*

   I'm sorry. I should have come sooner.

JANE. Yeah. You should.

   She relents. She shows him the pottery bowl.

Everything I pick up reminds me of something I want to forget.

Look at this.

I made it for my mum's birthday when I was seven. That should be a happy memory, shouldn't it?

RAY. I know it was hard for you. But in fairness, your mum was –

JANE. Don't try and excuse her!

RAY. Christ, Jane. Get over yourself. It's not all about you.

A beat.

JANE. Blimey. What's eating you?

RAY. Sorry. Nothing.

JANE. Not like you to be so crabby.

RAY. Yeah. No. Sorry.

JANE. What's it about then?

RAY. Nothing.

JANE. Nothing? Oh, right.

They work.

Why don't you tell me?

RAY. It's all just water under the bridge.

JANE. Bollocks.

RAY. Just leave it.

JANE. You're telling *me* to leave it?

RAY. Yes.

JANE. I'm guessing it's about Ana?

RAY. Jane, just –

JANE. Something to do with her mother? That's what Ana thinks. That there's something that you're not telling her.

RAY. It doesn't help anybody to talk about it.

JANE. So there is something.

RAY. For Christ's sake, Jane, drop it. Please.

JANE. Did she betray the guerrillas? Did she collaborate with the Government? What?

RAY. I don't want to talk about it, Jane!

JANE. Oh, for Christ's sake, Ray. You can't spend your whole life looking the other way when there's something nasty in the room.

RAY. She was going to leave me.

If you want to know.

JANE. Oh shit. I see.

RAY. Just before she got the diagnosis, she told me. She was going back to El Salvador with Ana.

JANE. I'm sorry. I didn't...

RAY. She wanted to be part of the struggle. She felt bad, living in London when everyone she knew back there was...

But I thought it was irresponsible, taking a young child back into a civil war.

JANE. You refused to go?

RAY. Ana was so little! It was scary out there. The situation was so volatile.

JANE. I suppose she felt it was her country, she wanted to –

RAY. Yes, but we'd seen enough, *I'd* seen enough, to know that –

They massacred whole villages. Thousands disappeared. People were thrown off bridges into rivers.

JANE. You were scared.

RAY. Yes I was scared! It was entirely appropriate to be scared.

JANE. I can see that.

RAY. I wanted to be a good father.

JANE. I know.

RAY. We have to protect our children from danger.

JANE. Ray –

RAY. My friend Luis was a *commandante*.

The security services got him.

He turned up, bound, in the river Lempa.

He would have been alive when they threw him off the bridge.

JANE. Shit.

RAY. His wife took her children and managed to get to Mexico.

We heard a death squad got her, two years later.

The CIA had told them where she was living.

Pause.

JANE. It is frightening.

But we can't be scared.

RAY. Don't you start.

JANE. Is that what Ana's saying?

RAY. It feels like a time warp. I'm having the same arguments with Ana I had with her mother.

JANE. Maybe you should try and talk to her about it.

RAY. She's beginning to despise me anyway. I don't want to make it worse.

JANE. It might make it better.

RAY. Isn't it better just not to know these painful things?

JANE. No.

RAY. Shit.

He produces a photo.

JANE. What's that?

RAY. Your plane.

He hands her the photo.

She looks at the photo. She looks at RAY.

JANE. Where did you take this?

RAY. Here. At the little airport.

A couple of weeks ago.

She embraces him.

JANE. God.

The British Government is in on it. They're helping the Americans.

She has another look at the picture.

They're letting them use our airports in return for... what? Information? Handling our own 'high-value detainees'.

Of course. Oh shit, why didn't I see it? It was staring me in the face.

When they rang me back, they wanted to know if I was from a UK agency.

They were expecting me to be from British security services.

I didn't see it.

This is even bigger than I thought.

Ray.

She goes to RAY *and kisses him on the mouth. They kiss. They're both surprised by how lovely it is.* RAY *breaks off.*

RAY. Hang on, Jane.

They recover themselves.

JANE. It's okay.

RAY. No. I mean – there's more.

JANE. More?

RAY. Listen. I think it's coming back. I asked Pete to call me if he heard about it coming in again.

JANE. It never occurred to me – a little place like that. Surrounded by sheep. The British involvement – of course…

RAY. And –

JANE. What?

RAY. He rang me this morning.

JANE. Go on.

RAY. About a plane.

JANE. What plane?

RAY. It's coming in tonight.

JANE. What plane? What is it?

RAY. I think you should come with me.

It's your plane.

It's changed its number, but it's the same one, I'm pretty sure.

JANE. How –?

RAY. Because it's coming from Cairo. En route to America.

JANE. God, Ray. You're good. You're really good.

He kisses her.

Scene Twenty

A dog is barking furiously. Mocking laughter in the distance.

A small airport, the perimeter fence, just before sunset. Birds are singing, sheep are bleating.

RAY. I think there's just enough light.

   The noise of a plane.

JANE. Give me those binoculars.

RAY. Here it comes.

JANE. Yes – that must be it.

   RAY *starts shooting pictures manically.* JANE *looks at him, then looks through the binoculars.*

   That's it, isn't it? That little jet? That's it?

   Jesus. I can't get them focused.

RAY. Okay.

JANE. Have you got the tail number? That's what we need, the tail number…

RAY. Got it. I've got it.

JANE. Okay. Jesus. Jesus.

   They watch.

RAY. It looks like the crew are going to disembark.

JANE. I can see them.

   I can see their faces.

   Those are the men who…

RAY. I've got the photos. They're heading for that car.

   The sound of the jet engines rises to deafening levels, there are bright lights in the darkness, a wall of sound and light.

Scene Twenty-One

MINA, *at home, is sorting through Amin's clothes.*

Scene Twenty-Two

RAY*'s house the next morning.* RAY *is asleep in bed.* JANE *enters quietly, goes over to him.*

JANE (*tender*).Wake up, Raymondo. I've brought you a cup of tea.

She laughs. She kisses him. A tender moment.

RAY. Have you been out?

JANE. Yes.

While you were sleeping, I've been busy.

The pilot's name is Brad Southern.

RAY. Who?

JANE. Brad Southern! Christ, you couldn't make it up, could you?

RAY. How did you find out?

JANE. The hotel receptionist was very obliging. Three US citizens checked in for one night. Including our friend Brad.

Rest stop, as you said, before the return journey.

RAY. How did you...?

JANE. What's the first thing people do after they check in?

RAY. Take a shower?

JANE. Phone home to say goodnight to the kiddies.

RAY. How do you know?

JANE. I guessed. That's what you'd have done.

RAY. Yes, but I'm a dad. These people are CIA operatives.

JANE. Special forces, actually. Area code 919. That's a number in Smithfield, North Carolina. Nice and handy for Fort Bragg.

RAY. How did you get that?

JANE. Printout of outgoing calls. But then, the great thing is, that Brad uses his real name for his home phone line. So I just had to do a search on the number. And then, abracadabra – Brad Southern turns out to be one Matthew Clarke. Age fifty-seven. Ex-US military. Flew planes in Vietnam. Look – here's a picture of him at his wedding.

He's the fucker flying the plane.

Look at where he's been flying to in the last couple of months.

Kabul.

Rabat.

Guantanamo.

It's an A to Z of torture destinations.

This guy, Matthew. He's done them all.

RAY. You're a very clever woman. You know that, don't you?

JANE. We've got them now. Not just them, not just Matthew Clarke and his ilk. This means we've got Blair. We've got Jack Straw. They're colluding in torture.

They're facilitating the torture shuttle-service.

RAY. You were right.

JANE *looks at him.*

JANE. I couldn't have done it without you.

RAY. Come here and take a compliment for once in your life.

She goes to him.

When do you have to file your story?

JANE. I've done it.

They kiss.

RAY. Do you feel okay… about this? About last night?

JANE. Right now I feel absolutely bloody fantastic, Ray. How do you feel?

He shrugs.

RAY. Shell-shocked. In a good way.

Scene Twenty-Three

The pub garden of The Plough. ANA *is off duty, sitting with* JANE.

JANE. Did Ray talk to you, about your mum?

ANA. Yes.

JANE. I'm sorry.

ANA. Thanks for, you know.

JANE. It must be a hard thing to find out.

ANA. It makes sense. Why he didn't want to talk about it.

It was great, your article.

JANE. Oh right. Yes. Page eight.

ANA. No. It was good.

JANE. Yeah, it was good. But… Page eight.

ANA. I've put the link on my blog. I've had loads of interest.

JANE. What?

ANA. Loads of people have read the article and posted comments on my blog. Have a look.

JANE. Do I get paid for every person who reads my article on your blog?

ANA. Do you have a website?

JANE. No.

ANA. You should. I can help you, if you want.

JANE. So now you want to help me? The poor old dinosaur.

ANA. In fact, it might be a kind of barter system I was thinking of.

JANE. You help me and I…? What?

ANA. This is kind of sensitive. I hope I can trust you with it?

JANE. I hope you can, too.

ANA. I've been contacted by this woman.

She says she works for the British forces in Iraq. Not sure if she's a soldier or an administrator. But she doesn't like what she's seeing, out there. She's sent me a whole load of documentation. And I'm a bit out of my depth.

JANE. What's she claiming to reveal?

ANA. The truth about how it's going out there. Not well, I think is the general idea.

She's got photos.

A pause.

JANE. You need to verify she is who she says she is.

You need to find out if her documents are genuine.

You need to make sure she's not just some crank with a grudge.

You need to make sure that nothing she's leaking is going to endanger anybody's life out there.

ANA. Okay, but how? Can you – can we...

Will you help me?

JANE. I'd be prepared to discuss some kind of deal.

Yes.

Scene Twenty-Four

A week or two later. MINA *at her home with* JANE.

MINA. I'm looking back at the last few weeks before he went, and remembering every detail, and suddenly I keep seeing clues. Clues that I missed.

He was always on the computer.

He was always angry.

We had a family party, and he got in to an argument – I wish I could remember what sparked it off – but I remember looking at him and thinking, 'God, who are you?'

JANE. Mina. You said you had something for me?

MINA. I felt he was pretending to be someone who he wasn't. He was pulling away from me. And I didn't know what to do.

JANE. You tried to talk to him.

MINA. I just wanted to stop him going.

Now, I just don't know.

JANE. You said you had a phone call?

MINA. Yes.

JANE. And? Who was it?

MINA. It was on my mobile. A number didn't come up. It said 'Blocked'.

JANE. Okay.

MINA. I answered.

JANE. And?

MINA. He said, 'It's me.'

JANE. 'It's me.' As in…?

MINA. I didn't recognise his voice. I said, 'Who?'

JANE. When was this, Mina?

MINA. And he said, 'It's me.' And I was thinking, 'Who's me? Who can this be?' It was as if my brain was working really slowly, and then I heard myself say, 'Amin?'

And he said, 'Yes.'

And I said it again, I said, 'Amin?'

And he said, 'Yes.' He said, 'I'm okay.'

And I said, 'Where are you?'

And he said, 'I'm coming home.'

He sounded odd. He didn't sound like him. He sounded sort of flat.

He said, 'I've been well treated. There was some mistake, when they picked me up. But they've told me that soon I'll be coming home.'

JANE. Wow.

When?

MINA. I don't know when. He said he'd call me.

JANE. You'll need to get hold of a really good lawyer.

MINA. He wouldn't say where he was.

JANE. He wasn't free to talk.

MINA. No. I suppose not.

JANE. He may be in a bad way. You should be prepared for that.

MINA *looks at her.*

I would really like to interview him, when he comes.

MINA. I told my family, what you thought.

They just thought I was mad.

They said I should face up to the fact that he'd left me.

They said I should get on with my life.

JANE. Well, you know what, Mina? He didn't leave you.

A beat.

What will you do?

MINA. I don't know.

She cries.

Scene Twenty-Five

MINA *is waiting at the airport, nervous and afraid. She sees him. She's shocked. She tries to hide her shock. She walks towards him.*

Scene Twenty-Six

RAY *and* JANE *in* JANE*'s mother's house, which has now been completely emptied.*

RAY. I used to love that little airport.

JANE. I'm sorry I've put you off your hobby.

RAY. It was time to move on.

I've decided to take Ana to El Salvador. Visit the places we visited.

JANE. That's good, Ray.

RAY. I should've done it before.

JANE. Better late than never.

How will that be for you?

RAY. It would be better, Jane, if you came with me.

JANE. What? Why me?

RAY. For a holiday. After we've done the family bit, Ana's going off travelling with her boyfriend. So you and me, we could…

JANE. I can't afford it, Ray.

RAY. Why don't you write about it? It's ten years since the end of the war. The FMLN is a mainstream political party now. We could try and trace some of the people I knew, find out what they're doing now. You could –

JANE. Do you know how interested the British public is in what's happening in El Salvador?

RAY. Yes, but –

JANE. I'd never be able to sell a story.

RAY. Forget work. When did you last have a holiday? The Pacific Ocean, Jane – I always thought you'd love it. It's phosphorescent at night, and warm, and the sound of it! It roars.

JANE. No, Ray.

RAY. We could travel on to Guatemala, up to Mexico.

A pause.

JANE. I don't think so, Ray. I'm sorry.

RAY. Just... a holiday, Jane? With me?

JANE. I'm sorry. I'm not –

You and me, I mean, that's not...

RAY. What d'you mean?

JANE. Look. I'm sorry. I didn't mean to mislead you. It's been nice, really nice, but –

RAY. But?

JANE. I never meant...

RAY. People shouldn't live their lives alone, Jane. I don't want to.

JANE. Sometimes it's better that way.

RAY. Ever since that night, we've both been happy, haven't we?

JANE. Just – sorry, Ray. Please. Don't.

RAY. That's it? Don't?

She shrugs.

There are moments in life, Jane, when you can – I dunno. Change course.

JANE. This isn't one of them, Ray.

RAY. It could be.

JANE. No, Ray. It's too late.

RAY. What do you mean?

JANE. Why didn't you *do* anything, back then? You knew what was going on at home. Why didn't you intervene?

RAY. What?

JANE. All you did was give me hot dinners. Why didn't you try and stop it?

RAY. Jane?

JANE. It's too late now, Ray. The damage is done. I've found a way to live my life. I'm not fine, but I'm okay. Just don't ask more of me than I can do.

Scene Twenty-Seven

JANE *and* MINA *at a table.*

JANE. Will he agree to talk to me?

MINA. He's not in any state to.

He has to be sedated.

He's…

JANE. Has he said anything? Has he said anything about his interrogators?

MINA. He can't talk about it. He just cries.

JANE. If I could just talk to him. For half an hour?

MINA. It's not good for him!

JANE *hands* MINA *a piece of paper with the flight logs on.*

She repeats the codes, it sounds meaningless. But as she repeats them, the words gradually suggest a journey, which she recognises.

KJNX – Johnston, North Carolina to KIAD, Washington, DC.

KIAD, Washington, DC to LEPA, Palma, Majorca to OPRN, Islamabad, Pakistan.

OPRN, Islamabad, Pakistan to OJAI, Amman, Jordan.

She sees Amin's journey mapped out.

JANE *turns on her digital recorder.*

This is where they took him, isn't it?

JANE. Yes.

MINA. This is…

Is this factual?

JANE. Yes.

MINA. I mean, it's all true?

JANE. Yes.

MINA. I didn't believe it.

She falters. She recovers.

Some of them were speaking Arabic. He thinks they might have been Jordanian.

JANE. Yes. How did they treat him?

MINA. They beat him, they hurt him.

And there were some Americans.

JANE. They asked him questions?

MINA. They kept him all alone. I don't know what the Americans did.

But they scared him. They really scared him.

JANE. I understand.

MINA. But the worst for him was the British man.

JANE. What?

MINA. He didn't see him. He was hooded. But when he heard the accent, he thought he'd be rescued. He thought the British had come to get him out of there.

JANE. A British official?

MINA. He just asked more questions.

JANE. You're sure about that?

MINA. Yes. I'm sure.

JANE. Thank you.

MINA. That's all I can tell you.

JANE. That's good. Thank you.

MINA. As soon as he's well enough, I'll ask him to talk to you.

JANE. Give him the flight logs for his journeys. It might help.

MINA. Thank you. Yes.

MINA notices JANE is holding more printouts.

What's that?

JANE. This is the flight logs of that plane, that took Amin.

These are all the other journeys it's taken over the last three years.

We know where the plane went.

We don't know, yet, who was onboard.

She hands her the paper.

She repeats the words, echoed by the rest of the cast, so we get the sense of hundreds of rendition flights, hundreds of unknown ghost prisoners.

MINA *and* VOICES. Johnson County to Dulles, Washington.

Dulles, Washington to Cairo, Egypt.

Cairo, Egypt to Stockholm, Sweden.

Stockholm, Sweden to Cairo, Egypt.

Islamabad, Pakistan to Rabat-Salé, Morocco.

Rabat-Salé, Morocco to Rome, Italy.

Rome, Italy to Amman, Jordan.

Amman, Jordon to Damascus, Syria.

Palma, Majorca to Skopje, Macedonia.

Skopje, Macedonia to Saddam International, Iraq.

Saddam International, Iraq to Kabul, Afghanistan.

Karachi, Pakistan to Amman, Jordan.

Amman, Jordan to Guantanamo Bay, Cuba.

Slow fade.

The End.

A Nick Hern Book

Blue Sky first published in Great Britain as a paperback original in 2012 by Nick Hern Books Limited, The Glasshouse, 49a Goldhawk Road, London W12 8QP, in association with Pentabus Theatre

Blue Sky copyright © 2012 Clare Bayley

Clare Bayley has asserted her right to be identified as the author of this work

Cover photograph by Richard Stanton
Cover design by Ned Hoste, 2H

Typeset by Nick Hern Books, London
Printed in Great Britain by Mimeo Ltd, Huntingdon, Cambridgeshire PE29 6XX

A CIP catalogue record for this book is available from the British Library

ISBN   978 1 84842 302 2